W9-CUA-305

Andreas Capellanus

THE ART OF COURTLY LOVE

Translated by
JOHN JAY PARRY

Edited and abridged by
FREDERICK W. LOCKE
Stanford University

FREDERICK UNGAR PUBLISHING CO.
NEW YORK

MILESTONES
OF THOUGHT
in the History of Ideas

General Editor
F. W. STROTHMANN
Stanford University

Seventeenth Printing, 1980

Printed in the United States of America

ISBN 0-8044-6075-2

Library of Congress Catalog Card Number 56-12400

INTRODUCTION

Andreas Capellanus and the Doctrine of Courtly Love

MUCH HAS happened to change our views of the Middle Ages since the publication of Will Durant's *History of Philosophy*. It will be recalled that in his first edition Mr. Durant saw fit to pass over medieval philosophy as completely unworthy of serious examination. In doing so he was illustrating most eloquently the prevalent attitude towards the ten centuries which had been hidden away in shame between Antiquity and Modernity. And though at this late date it would be almost impossible to change the name, the term "Middle Ages" itself has had no small influence upon our conception of a vast period of European history which has not been so homogeneous as we had been led to believe.

Today the situation is quite different. There is at the present time a very lively interest in the Middle Ages, a growing awareness of the significance of its contributions to literature, art, music, and thought. It is no longer possible to characterize the period between 500 and 1500 as the Dark Ages. There has been, indeed, much talk in recent years of a Renaissance of the Twelfth Century, a kind of proto-renaissance, wherein are to be detected symptoms of that intellectual and artistic unrest which culminated in the High Renaissance of the sixteenth century. All of our large universities offer courses in Medieval Latin and the vernacular languages and literatures of the older period. There has also been a renewed interest in the study of Dante and the Troubadours, and through the work of such scholars as Étienne Gilson there has come about such an interest in medieval philosophy that at least one American university has at this time a chair devoted to this subject. In the area of medieval art the books of Emile Mâle and Joan Evans have awakened a new kind of appreciation and understanding of Romanesque and Gothic style.

The publication of the treatise of Andreas Capellanus in the "Milestones of Thought" series requires, therefore, no defense. The work itself, however, may stand in need of certain background information which will better enable the reader to gain a very necessary perspective.

In the eyes of Capellanus, passionate love is an ennobling force. As a matter of fact, it is the source of all manly virtues. This view of passionate love between the sexes is alien to the Greeks and the Romans. Whenever passionate love manifests itself in the literature of Antiquity, it is either regarded as a chastisement inflicted on men by the gods—as in Euripides, to whom the love of Phaedra for Hippolytus is a punishment visited upon the young man for his neglect of Aphrodite—or—as in the case of Ovid—it is viewed simply as sensual gratification.

When, therefore, Capellanus, expressing the ideals of the social group to which he belonged, depicts passionate love as an ennobling experience, we must recognize this evaluation as something totally new; and from a social point of view we must even recognize it as revolutionary. For when a passionate lover obediently subjects himself to the beloved lady as to his "mistress," he grants to this lady a status which women simply did not enjoy either in Antiquity or in the early Middle Ages.

In spite of the Christian form of society, it would be misleading indeed to conceive of a status for women during the early Middle Ages which was at all comparable to that of the modern American woman. Women are not important, for instance, in the old French Epics. In the eyes of medieval men, this is a man's world, and it is only the deeds of men, particularly of warriors, that are worthy of being chronicled. Unless a woman in the older period happens to be a saint, she is not mentioned at any length; and there is no concern with passionate love between the sexes, but rather, as in Antiquity, with the friendship of man for man, of warrior for warrior, as classically illustrated in the devotion of Roland and Olivier for each other in "The Song of Roland."

Outside of marriage, women might be used to alleviate concupiscence; and in the married state, recommended by St. Paul because it is better to marry than to burn, she had the additional function of being a childbearer and a housekeeper, hardly that of a companion with a status equal to that of men. From the very earliest period of Christianity, passionate love was deplored; and not until the time of Albertus Magnus and Thomas Aquinas in the thirteenth century did the theologians begin to mitigate their contention that passionate love towards even one's wife was sinful.

Behind this medieval attitude towards women was a monastic tradition whose influence upon letters and institutions cannot be overestimated. The angry denunciation against the perennial Eve is a cry that is heard throughout the period: every woman is *Eva rediviva,* the personification of the temptress through whom man originally fell from innocence.

According to the record, a new conception of love appeared at the beginning of the twelfth century, a conception which was eventually to change the prevalent attitude toward women. This new attitude showed itself at first exclusively among the members of the aristocratic class in the south of France, and even when it moved north there is no indication that it was responsible for any marked change in attitude within the lower classes of society. The initial symptoms of this change in the aristocracy's attitude toward love are noticed in the south of France in the person of Guillaume IX, duke of Poitiers (1071-1127), who is the first of the known Troubadours. But it is not until we come to Bernart de Ventadorn (1148-1195) that the radically new theme of Provençal lyric poetry, i.e., Courtly Love, manifests its real character.

The term *amour courtois,* or Courtly Love, is of modern origin. It was first applied in 1883 by the great French medievalist Gaston Paris in an attempt to coin a term for this new form of love which makes such a decided break with previous forms and which appears for the first time in Europe among the Troubadours of Provence.

The poetry of the Troubadours and that of the Trouvères in the north of France speaks of a love which, while essentially adulterous, inspires the man with nobility of character and offers him, through the beloved, a transcendent experience. It is this power of transformation which, more than anything else, constitutes the distinguishing characteristic of Courtly Love, a love which both as a literary theme and as a social ideal is something entirely new on the European scene, and from which our modern notions of romantic love derive in a large measure. Without Courtly Love, the tragic passionate love of the modern novel and theatre would be difficult to explain. Courtly Love has influenced men's deepest attitude toward the other sex, our unquestioned sense of courtesy in the West, our persistent, if socially crystallized, deference toward women. Courtly Love is also responsible for the "democratization" of relations between man and woman, inasmuch as not social position but intrinsic worth determined the mutual acceptability of the partners according to the courtly code.

Though scholars have traced many of the lines of transmission of Troubadour poetry and have shown most clearly the sources of many of the forms of Provençal verse, the origins of the phenomenon of Courtly Love still remain wrapped in mystery. Up to the present, there is no agreement as to how it actually started or whence it derives. Attempts have been made to find its origins in Ovid, in Arabic philosophy, in Neo-Platonism, in the mystical writings of Christians and Moslems, and in the heresy of the Albigensians.

Whatever may be the origin of what has come to be called Courtly Love, it is the codification of its principles that is the subject of *The Art of Courtly Love* (*De arte honeste amandi*), written some time between 1174 and 1186 by Andreas Capellanus. His work, like that of the *Art Poétique* of Boileau, which appeared after the classical movement of the seventeenth century had come to flower, is descriptive, not prescriptive: it does not propose anything new, but rather codifies what was already in existence.

There are also signs that its author cannot accept the code he sets forth. The evidence for this is in the strange Third Book which flatly contradicts the principles set up in the first two. Is this third book an apology offered by the Christian conscience because of the unacceptability of Courtly Love? We do not know.

Only one thing is certain. As a description of the theory of Courtly Love, *The Art of Courtly Love* is an invaluable document and among the most provocative which have come down from the period of the High Middle Ages.

F.W.L.

SELECTED BIBLIOGRAPHY

Andreae Capellani regii Francorum De amore libri tres.
Recensuit E. Trojel. Havniae [Copenhagen] in Libraria
Gandiana, 1892.
Andreae Capellani regii Francorum De amore libri tres.
Text llatí publicat per Amadeu Pagès. Castelló de la
Plana [Sociedad Castellonense de Cultura], 1929.
Denomy, A. J. *The Heresy of Courtly Love*. New York:
Macmillan Company, 1947.
Lewis, C. S. *The Allegory of Love*. London: Oxford University Press, 1948.

NOTE

The translation from which this text has been edited is that of the late Professor John Jay Parry, *The Art of Courtly Love,* Columbia University Press, 1941. Changes have been made in Professor Parry's translation only at those points where new connections had to be established through the excerpting of material, or when it was deemed advisable to emend a colloquial expression which is not any more current. For the use of Professor Parry's translation we acknowledge the kind permission of Columbia University Press.

The chapter numbering of the Parry edition has been changed to conform with the sequence of the selections here presented.

CONTENTS

BOOK THREE

The Rejection of Love   44

AUTHOR'S PREFACE

I am greatly impelled by the continual urging of my love for you, my revered friend Walter, to make known by word of mouth and to teach you by my writings the way in which a state of love between two lovers may be kept unharmed and likewise how those who do not love may get rid of the darts of Venus that are fixed in their hearts.

You tell me that you are a new recruit of Love, and, having recently been wounded by an arrow of his, you do not know how to manage your horse's reins properly and you cannot find any cure for yourself. How serious this is and how it troubles my soul no words of mine can make clear to you. For I know, having learned from experience, that it does not do the man who owes obedience to Venus's service any good to give careful thought to anything except how he may always be doing something that will entangle him more firmly in his chains; he thinks he has nothing good except what may wholly please his love.

Therefore, although it does not seem expedient to devote oneself to things of this kind or fitting for any prudent man to engage in this kind of hunting, nevertheless, because of the affection I have for you I can by no means refuse your request; because I know clearer than day that after you have learned the art of love your progress in it will be more cautious, in so far as I can I shall comply with your desire.

BOOK ONE

Introduction to the Treatise on Love

We must first consider what love is, whence it gets its name, what the effect of love is, between what persons love may exist, how it may be acquired, retained, increased, decreased, and ended, what are the signs that one's love is returned, and what one of the lovers ought to do if the other is unfaithful.

CHAPTER I

What Love Is

Love is a certain inborn suffering derived from the sight of and excessive meditation upon the beauty of the opposite sex, which causes each one to wish above all things the embraces of the other and by common desire to carry out all of love's precepts in the other's embrace.

That love is suffering is easy to see, for before the love becomes equally balanced on both sides there is no torment greater, since the lover is always in fear that his love may not gain its desire and that he is wasting his efforts. He fears, too, that rumors of it may get abroad, and he fears everything that might harm it in any way, for before things are perfected a slight disturbance often spoils them. If he is a poor man, he also fears that the woman may scorn his poverty; if he is ugly, he fears that she may despise his lack of beauty or may give her love to a more handsome man; if he is rich, he fears that his parsimony in the past may stand in his way. To tell the truth, no one can number the fears of one single lover. This kind of love, then, is a suffering which is felt by only one of the persons and may be called "single love." But even after both are in love the fears that arise are just as great, for each of the lovers fears that what he has acquired with so much effort may be lost through the effort of someone else, which is certainly much worse for a man than if, having no hope, he sees that his efforts are accomplishing nothing, for it is worse to lose the things you are seeking than to be deprived of a gain you merely hope for. The lover fears, too, that he may offend his loved one in some way; indeed he fears so many things that it would be difficult to tell them.

That this suffering is inborn I shall show you clearly, because if you will look at the truth and distinguish carefully you will see that it does not arise out of any action; only from the reflection of the mind upon what it sees does this suffering come. For when a man sees some woman fit for love and shaped according to his taste, he begins at once to lust after her in his heart; then the more he thinks about her the more he burns with love, until he comes to a fuller meditation. Presently he begins to think about the fashioning of the woman and to differentiate her limbs, to think about what she does, and to pry into the secrets of her body, and he desires to put each part of it to the fullest use. Then after he has come to this complete meditation, love cannot hold the reins, but he proceeds at once to action; straightway he strives to get a helper to find an intermediary. He begins to plan how he may find favor with her, and he begins to seek a place and a time opportune for talking; he looks upon a brief hour as a very long year, because he cannot do anything fast enough to suit his eager mind. It is well known that many things happen to him in this manner. This inborn suffering comes, therefore, from seeing and meditating. Not every kind of meditation can be the cause of love, an excessive one is required; for a restrained thought does not, as a rule, return to the mind, and so love cannot arise from it.

CHAPTER II

Between What Persons Love May Exist

Now, in love you should note first of all that love cannot exist except between persons of opposite sexes. Between two men or two women love can find no place, for we see that two persons of the same sex are not at all fitted for giving each other the exchanges of love or for practicing the acts natural to it. Whatever nature forbids, love is ashamed to accept.

CHAPTER III

What the Effect of Love Is ~ennobling

Now it is the effect of love that a true lover cannot be degraded with any avarice. Love causes a rough and un-couth man to be distinguished for his handsomeness; it can endow a man even of the humblest birth with nobility of character; it blesses the proud with humility; and the man in love becomes accustomed to performing many services gracefully for everyone. O what a wonderful thing is love, which makes a man shine with so many virtues and teaches everyone, no matter who he is, so many good traits of char-acter! There is another thing about love that we should not praise in few words: it adorns a man, so to speak, with the virtue of chastity, because he who shines with the light of one love can hardly think of embracing another woman, even a beautiful one. For when he thinks deeply of his be-loved the sight of any other woman seems to his mind rough and rude.

CHAPTER IV

What Persons Are Fit for Love

We must now see what persons are fit to bear the arms of love. You should know that everyone of sound mind who is capable of doing the work of Venus may be wounded by one of love's arrows unless prevented by age, or blindness, or excess of passion.

An excess of passion is a bar to love, because there are men who are slaves to such passionate desire that they cannot be held in the bonds of love—men who, after they have thought long about some woman or even enjoyed her, when they see another woman straightway desire her embraces, and they forget about the services they have received from their first love and they feel no gratitude for them. Men of this kind lust after every woman they see; their love is like that of a shameless dog. They should rather, I believe, be compared to asses, for they are moved only by that low nature which shows that men are on the level of the other animals rather than by that true nature which sets us apart from all the other animals by the difference of reason.

CHAPTER V

In What Manner Love May Be Acquired, and in How Many Ways

It remains next to be seen in what ways love may be acquired.

A beautiful figure wins love with very little effort, especially when the lover who is sought is simple, for a simple lover thinks that there is nothing to look for in one's beloved besides a beautiful figure and face and a body well cared for.

But a wise woman will seek as a lover a man of praiseworthy character—not one who anoints himself all over like a woman or makes a rite of the care of the body, for it does not go with a masculine figure to adorn oneself in womanly fashion or to be devoted to the care of the body.

Likewise, if you see a woman too heavily rouged you will not be taken in by her beauty unless you have already discovered that she is good company besides, since a woman who puts all her reliance on her rouge usually doesn't have any particular gifts of character. As I said about men, so with women—I believe you should not seek for beauty so much as for excellence of character. For since all of us human beings are derived originally from the same stock and all naturally claim the same ancestor, it was not beauty or care of the body or even abundance of possessions, but excellence of character alone which first made a distinction of nobility among men and led to the difference of class.

Character alone, then, is worthy of the crown of love. Many times fluency of speech will incline to love the hearts of those who do not love, for an elaborate line of talk on the part of the lover usually sets love's arrows a-flying and creates a presumption in favor of the excellent character of the speaker. How this may be I shall try to show you as briefly as I can.

To this end I shall first explain to you that one woman belongs to the middle class, a second to the simple nobility, and a third to the higher nobility. So it is with men: one is of the middle class, another of the nobility, a third of the higher nobility, and a fourth of the very highest nobility. What I mean by a woman of the middle class is clear enough to you; a noblewoman is one descended from an untitled nobleman [vavasor] or a lord, or is the wife of one of these, while a woman of the higher nobility is descended from great lords. The same rules apply to men, except that a man married to a woman of higher or lower rank than himself does not change his rank. A married woman changes her status to match that of her husband, but a man can never change his nobility by marriage. In addition, among men we find one rank more than among women, since there is a man more noble than any of these, that is, the clerk.

FIRST DIALOGUE

*A man of the middle class speaks with a woman
of the same class.*

THE MAN SAYS: "When the Divine Being made you there was nothing that He left undone. I know that there is no defect in your beauty, none in your good sense, none in you at all except, it seems to me, that you have enriched no one by your love. I marvel greatly that Love permits so beautiful and so sensible a woman to serve for long outside his camp. If you should take service with Love, blessed above all others will that man be whom you shall crown with your love! Now if I, by my merits, might be worthy of such an honor, no lover in the world could really be compared with me."

THE WOMAN SAYS: "You seem to be lying, since although I do not have a beautiful figure you extol me as beautiful beyond all other women and although I lack the ornament of wisdom you praise my good sense. The very highest wisdom ought not to be required of a woman descended from the middle class."

THE MAN SAYS: "It is a habit of wise people never to admit with their own mouths their good looks or their good character, and by so doing they clearly show their character, because prudent people guard their words so carefully that no one may have reason to apply to them that common proverb which runs, 'All praise is filthy in one's own mouth.' You, like a wise woman, not wishing to fall foul of this saying, leave all praise of you to others; but there are so many who do praise you that it would never be right to say that one of them meant to lie. Even those who do not love you for the sake of your family are, I know, diligent in singing your praises. And besides, if you think you are not beautiful, you should believe that I must really be in love, since to me your beauty excels that of all other women; and love makes even an ugly woman seem very beautiful to her lover. You said, too, that you come of a humble family. But this shows that you are much more deserving of praise and blessed with greater nobility, since yours does not come from your descent or from your ancestors, but good character and good manners alone have given to you a more worthy kind of nobility. In the beginning the same nature created all men, and to this day they would have remained equal had not greatness of soul and worth of character commenced to set men apart from each other by the inequality of nobility."

THE WOMAN SAYS: "If I am as noble as you are trying to make out, you, being a man of the middle class, should seek the love of some woman of the same class, while I look for a noble lover to match my noble status; for nobility and commonalty do not go well together or dwell in the same abode."

THE MAN SAYS: "Your answer would seem good enough if it were only in women that a lowly birth might be ennobled by excellence of character. But since an excellent character makes noble not only women but men also, you are perhaps wrong in refusing me your love, since my manners, too, may illumine me with the virtue of nobility. Your first concern should be whether I lack refined manners, and if you find my status higher than you would naturally expect, you ought not deprive me of the hope of your love. For one whose nobility is that of character it is more proper to choose a lover whose nobility is of the same kind than one who is high-born but unmannerly. Indeed, if you should find a man who is distinguished by both kinds of nobility, it would be better to take as a lover the man whose only nobility is that of character. For the one gets his nobility from his ancient stock and from his noble father and derives it as a sort of inheritance from those from whom he gets his being; but the other gets his nobility only from himself, and what he takes is not derived from his family tree, but springs only from the best qualities of his mind. You should therefore approve the second man's nobility more than that of the other. For I notice that we consider more worthy of praise and reward that king who received a small realm from his ancestors and afterwards by his virtuous rule brought countless nations under his sway than the king who retains undisturbed the many kingdoms which he inherited. If, therefore, you recognize that I enjoy nobility of manners, incline your excellence toward me and give me at least the hope of your love, which I have so long desired, so that I may live; for there is no hope of saving me if you cause me to despair of your love."

SECOND DIALOGUE

A man of the middle class speaks with a woman of the nobility.

The Man Says: "I know well that Love is not in the habit of differentiating men with titles of distinction, but that he obligates all equally to serve in his army, making no exceptions for beauty or birth and making no distinctions of sex or of inequality of family, considering only this, whether anybody is fit to bear Love's armor. Love is a thing that copies Nature herself, and so lovers ought to make no more distinction between classes of men than Love himself does. Just as love inflames men of all classes, so lovers should draw no distinctions of rank, but consider only whether the man who asks for love has been wounded by Love. Supported by this unanswerable argument, I may select for my beloved any woman I choose so long as I have no depravity of character to debase me."

The Woman Says: "Who are you that ask for such great gifts? I know well enough what you look like, and the family you come from is obvious. But where can one find greater effrontery than in a man who for the space of a whole week devotes all his efforts to the various gains of business and then on the seventh day, his day of rest, tries to enjoy the gifts of love and to dishonor Love's commands and confound the distinctions of classes established among men from of old? It is not without cause or reason that this distinction of rank has been found among men from the very beginning; it is so that every man will stay within the bounds of his own class and be content with all things therein and never presume to arrogate to himself the things that were naturally set aside as belonging to a higher class, but will leave them severely alone. Who are you, then, to try to defile such ancient statutes and under the pretense of love to attempt to subvert the precepts of our ancestors and so presumptuously go beyond the limits of your own class?"

THE MAN SAYS: "Although I am repulsed by what you say, still as long as I live I shall not give up the idea of your love, because even if I am never to get the result I hope for, the mere hope I have gained from the greatness of my heart will cause my body to lead a tranquil life, and ultimately, perhaps, God will put into your mind a cure for my pain."

THE WOMAN SAYS: "May God give you a reward suited to your effort."

THE MAN SAYS: "That word alone shows me that my hope is bearing fruit, and I pray to God that you may always be interested in the care of my health and that my sails may find a quiet haven."

THIRD DIALOGUE

*A man of the middle class speaks with
a woman of the higher nobility.*

If a man of the middle class seeks the love of a woman of the higher nobility, he ought to have a most excellent character, for in order that a man of this class may prove worthy of the love of a woman of the higher nobility he must be a man with innumerable good things to his credit, one whom uncounted good deeds extol. It would seem a very great shame and a cause of reproach for a noblewoman to pass over the upper and the intermediate ranks and take a lover from the lower class unless good character in overwhelming quantity makes up for the lack of nobility. For it would not seem unreasonable to any sensible people that one could find in the lowest class good and excellent men, worthy of the love of a woman of such high rank, while in the upper classes no worthy man could be found, but all had to be rejected as of inferior quality. This is what you are told by the general rule of the logicians, which says, "If what appears more present is not present, neither will that which is believed less be." A man of the middle class must therefore greatly excel in character all the men of the two noble classes in order to deserve the love of a woman of the higher nobility, for no matter how worthy any commoner may be, it seems very much out of place if a countess or a marchioness or any woman of the same or a higher rank gives her love to a man of the middle class, and even the lower classes look upon it as a lowering and a demeaning of herself. The first thing people will think is that she does it out of too great an abundance of passion (a thing which I shall show later is wholly reprehensible), unless the man's character is so well known as to remove the suspicion of that. Well, then, isn't it proper that a woman of the higher nobility should give her love to a commoner if she finds him excellent in every way? I answer that if she finds anyone in the classes above him who is more worthy or as worthy, she ought to prefer the love of that man; but if she doesn't find any such person in these classes, then she should not reject the commoner.

Therefore a man of the middle class may be chosen in love by a woman of the higher nobility if after long probation he is found to be worthy. In that case he may make some such speech as the following:

"It doesn't seem at all profitable to dwell very much

on the praise of your person, for your character and your beauty echo through widely separated parts of the world, and, furthermore, praise uttered in the presence of the person praised seems to have the appearance of clever flattery. For the present, then, it is my intention, and the principal object which brings me here to you, to offer you myself and my services and to beg earnestly that Your Grace may see fit to accept them. And I beseech God in heaven that of His grace He may grant me to do those things which are wholly pleasing to your desire."

THE WOMAN SAYS: "You seem to have a reasonable defense, but what good deeds glorify you, what sort of character makes you worthy to obtain what you ask, I have never heard. He who asks for the love of an honorable woman, especially one of the upper nobility, ought to be of great fame and of all courtliness; but of you lofty fame seems to be perfectly silent. First, therefore, you should strive to do such things as deserve the reward which you ask, so that your request may not be considered too impudent."

THE MAN SAYS: "The height of courtesy seems to be contained in your remarks, in which you are so clearly concerned that all my actions should be laudable. And so, since I see that you are thoroughly instructed in the art of love, I ask you to give me a lesson—that is, I ask that Your Grace may see fit to teach me those things that are specially demanded in love, those which make a man most worthy of being loved, because after I have been instructed I shall have no defense for any mistakes I make and no opportunity to excuse myself. Since all courtesy comes from the plentiful stream of Love and to this generous lord should be credited the beginning of all good deeds and the carrying out to the end of every good, and since I am still inexperienced in love and ignorant of the subject, it is no wonder that I know nothing of what he can do and that I urgently seek to be taught his precepts; because what anyone desires with all his mind he begs for vehemently and receives with eagerness."

THE WOMAN SAYS: "You seem to be upsetting the natural order and course of things, since first you ask for love and then you show yourself in every way unworthy of it by asking like a raw recruit to be trained in the science of love. But since it would seem to set a shameful precedent, one prompted by avarice, if those who have experience were to deny their lessons to those who have not and ask to be taught, you will without a doubt obtain the grant of our instruction; and if you will pay careful attention to our words, before you leave you will be fully informed on the subjects you ask about.

"Well then, the man who would be considered worthy to serve in Love's army must not be in the least avaricious, but very generous; he must, in fact, give generously to as many people as he can. When he sees that money is needed, especially by noblemen and men of character, and when he thinks that his gifts would be helpful to anybody, he ought not wait to be urged, for a gift made in answer to a request seems dearly bought.

"And if he has a lord, he should offer him due respect. He should utter no word of blasphemy against God and His saints; he should show himself humble to all and should stand ready to serve everybody. He ought never speak a word in disparagement of any man, since those who speak evil may not remain within the threshold of courtesy. He ought not utter falsehood in praise of the wicked, but he should if possible make them better by secret reproofs. If he thinks that they remain wholly incorrigible, he should consider them stiff-necked and banish them from his company lest he be considered, and rightly, a promoter and a sharer of the error. He ought never mock anyone, especially the wretched, and he should not be quarrelsome or ready to take part in disputes; but he should be, so far as possible, a composer of differences. In the presence of women he should be moderate about his laughter, because, according to Solomon's saying, too much laughter is a sign of foolishness; and clever women are in the habit of turning away fools and unwise men in contempt or of eluding them beautifully. Great prudence is necessary in the management of a love affair and diligence in all one does.

"He ought to frequent assemblies of great men and to visit great courts. He should be moderate about indulging in games of dice. He should gladly call to mind and take to heart the great deeds of the men of old. He ought to be courageous in battle and hardy against his enemies, wise, cautious, and clever.

"He should not be a lover of several women at the same time, but for the sake of one he should be a devoted servant of all.

"He should devote only a moderate amount of care to the adornment of his person and should show himself wise and tractable and pleasant to everybody, although some men have the idea that women like it very much if they utter foolish, almost crazy, remarks and act like madmen.

"He should be careful, too, not to utter falsehoods and should take care not to talk too much or to keep silent too much. He should not be too quick and sudden about making promises, because the man who is good-natured about making promises will be slow to keep them, and the man who is too ready to make them gets little credit.

"He should not utter harmful or shameful or mocking words against God's clergy or monks or any person connected with a religious house, but should always and everywhere render them due honor with all his strength and with all his mind, for the sake of Him whose service they perform. He ought to go to church frequently and there listen gladly to those who are constantly celebrating ˋthe divine service, although some men very foolishly believe that the women like it if they despise everything connected with the Church. He ought to be truthful in everything he says and never envy any man's renown. I have presented to you briefly the main points. If you have listened attentively to them and will be careful to practice them, you will be found worthy to plead in the court of Love."

SEVENTH DIALOGUE

*A man of the higher nobility speaks with a
woman of the simple nobility.*

When a man of the higher nobility addresses a woman
of the simple nobility, let him use the same speeches that
a nobleman and a man of the higher nobility use with a
woman of the middle class, except that part dealing with the
commendation of birth, and he must not boast very much
of the fact that he is noble. In addition he might begin with
this formula:

"I ought to give God greater thanks than any other
living man in the whole world because it is now granted me
to see with my eyes what my soul has desired above all else
to see, and I believe that God has granted it to me because
of my great longing and because He has seen fit to hear
the prayers of my importunate supplication. For not an hour
of the day or night could pass that I did not earnestly pray
God to grant me the boon of seeing you near me in the
flesh. It is no wonder that I was driven by so great an impulse to see you and was tormented by so great a desire,
since the whole world extols your virtue and your wisdom,
and in the farthest parts of the world courts are fed upon
the tale of your goodness just as though it were a sort of
tangible food. And now I know in very truth that a human
tongue is not able to tell the tale of your beauty and your
prudence or a human mind to imagine it. And so the mighty
desire, which I already had, of seeing you and serving you
has greatly increased and will increase still more."

The Woman Says: "We are separated by too wide and
too rough an expanse of country to be able to offer each
other love's solaces or to find proper opportunities for meet-
ing. Lovers who live near together can cure each other of
the torments that come from love, can help each other in
their common sufferings, and can nourish their love by
mutual exchanges and efforts; those, however, who are far

apart cannot perceive each other's pains, but each one has to relieve his own trouble and cure his own torments. So it seems that our love should go no further, because Love's rule teaches us that the daily sight of each other makes lovers love more ardently, while I can see on the other hand that by reason of distance love decreases and fails, and therefore everybody should try to find a lover who lives near by."

THE MAN SAYS: "You are troubling yourself to say what seems to be against all reason, for all men know that if one gets easily what he desires he holds it cheap and what formerly he longed for with his whole heart he now considers worthless. On the other hand, whenever the possession of some good thing is postponed by the difficulty of getting it, we desire it more eagerly and put forth a greater effort to keep it. Therefore if one has difficulty in obtaining the embraces of one's lover and obtains them rarely, the lovers are bound to each other in more ardent chains of love and their souls are linked together in heavier and closer bonds of affection. For constancy is made perfect amid the waves that buffet it, and perseverance is clearly seen in adversities. Rest seems sweeter to a man who is wearied by many labors than to one who lives in continual idleness, and a new-found shade seems to offer more to one who is burdened by the heat than to one who has been constantly in air of a moderate temperature. It is not one of Love's rules, as you said it was, that when lovers seldom meet the strength of their love is weakened, since we find it false and misleading. Therefore you cannot properly refuse me your love with the excuse of the long and difficult distance between us, but you should gratify me rather than someone who lives near by; besides, it is easier to conceal a love affair when the lovers do not meet than when they converse frequently with each other."

THE WOMAN SAYS: "So far as hiding one's love goes, I do not think there is any choice between a distant lover and one who is present. If the lover proves to be wise and

clever it doesn't matter whether he is far from his beloved
or near her, he will so govern his actions and his will that
no one can guess the secrets of their love; on the other hand
a foolish lover, whether far or near, can never conceal the
secrets of his love. Your argument must therefore fall before
this most obvious one on the other side. Besides there is
another fact, by no means trivial, which keeps me from
loving you. I have a husband who is greatly distinguished
by his nobility, his good breeding, and his good character,
and it would be wicked for me to violate his bed or submit
to the embraces of any other man, since I know that he
loves me with his whole heart and I am bound to him with
all the devotion of mine. The laws themselves bid me refrain
from loving another man when I am blessed with such a
reward for my love."

THE MAN SAYS: "I admit it is true that your husband
is a very worthy man and that he is more blest than any
man in the world because he has been worthy to have the
joy of embracing Your Highness. But I am greatly surprised
that you wish to misapply the term 'love' to that marital
affection which husband and wife are expected to feel for
each other after marriage, since everybody knows that love
can have no place between husband and wife. They may be
bound to each other by a great and immoderate affection,
but their feeling cannot take the place of love, because it
cannot fit under the true definition of love. For what is love
but an inordinate desire to receive passionately a furtive
and hidden embrace? But what embrace between husband
and wife can be furtive, I ask you, since they may be said
to belong to each other and may satisfy each other's desires
without fear that anybody will object.

"But there is another reason why husband and wife cannot love each other and that is that the very substance of
love, without which true love cannot exist—I mean jealousy
—is in such a case very much frowned upon and they should
avoid it like the pestilence; but lovers should always welcome
it as the mother and the nurse of love. From this you may

see clearly that love cannot possibly flourish between you and your husband. Therefore, since every woman of character ought to love, prudently, you can without doing yourself any harm accept the prayers of a suppliant and endow your suitor with your love."

THE WOMAN SAYS: "You are trying to take under your protection what all men from early times down have agreed to consider very reprehensible and to reject as hateful. For who can rightly commend envious jealousy or speak in favor of it, since jealousy is nothing but a shameful and evil suspicion of a woman? God forbid, therefore, that any worthy man should feel jealous about anyone, since this proves hostile to every prudent person and throughout the world is hated by everybody good. You are trying also, under cover of defining love, to condemn love between husband and wife, saying that their embraces cannot be furtive, since without fear that anyone may object they can fulfill each other's desires. But if you understood the definition correctly it could not interfere with love between husband and wife, for the expression 'hidden embraces' is simply an explanation in different words of the preceding one, and there seems to be no impossibility in husband and wife giving each other hidden embraces, even though they can do so without the least fear that anybody may raise an objection. Everyone should choose that love which may be fostered by security for continual embraces and, what is more, can be practiced every day without any sin. I ought therefore to choose a man to enjoy my embraces who can be to me both husband and lover, because, no matter what the definition of love may say, love seems to be nothing but a great desire to enjoy carnal pleasure with someone, and nothing prevents this feeling existing between husband and wife."

THE MAN SAYS: "If the theory of love were perfectly clear to you and Love's dart had ever touched you, your own feelings would have shown you that love cannot exist without jealousy, because, as I have already told you in more detail, jealousy between lovers is commended by every man

who is experienced in love, while between husband and
wife it is condemned throughout the world; the reason for
this will be perfectly clear from a description of jealousy.
Now jealousy is a true emotion whereby we greatly fear that
the substance of our love may be weakened by some defect
in serving the desires of our beloved, and it is an anxiety
lest our love may not be returned.

"We find many, however, who are deceived in this matter and say falsely that a shameful suspicion is jealousy,
just as many often make the mistake of saying that an alloy
of silver and lead is the finest silver. Wherefore not a few
being ignorant of the origin and description of jealousy, are
often deceived and led into the gravest error. For even between persons who are not married this false jealousy may
find a place and then they are no longer called 'lovers' but
'gentleman friend' and 'lady friend.' As for what you tried
to prove by your answer—that the love which can be practiced without sin is far preferable—that, apparently, cannot
stand. For whatever solaces married people extend to each
other beyond what are inspired by the desire for offspring or
the payment of the marriage debt, cannot be free from sin,
and the punishment is always greater when the use of a holy
thing is perverted by misuse than if we practice the ordinary
abuses. It is a more serious offense in a wife than in another
woman, for the too ardent lover, as we are taught by the
apostolic law, is considered an adulterer with his own wife."

EIGHTH DIALOGUE

*A man of the higher nobility speaks with a woman
of the same class.*

THE WOMAN SAYS: "I know that women should be the
cause and origin of good things, that they should, of course,
receive everybody with a joyful face and give him a courteous reception, and that they should speak to each one words
appropriate to his condition and should clearly persuade

every man to do courteous deeds and to avoid everything that has the appearance of boorishness and not to be so tenacious of his own property as to blacken his good name. But to show love is gravely to offend God and to prepare for many the perils of death. And besides it seems to bring innumerable pains to the lovers themselves and to cause them constant torments every day.

THE MAN SAYS: "If you choose to serve God alone, you must give up all worldly things and contemplate only the mysteries of the Heavenly Country, for God has not wished that anybody should keep his right foot on earth and his left foot in heaven, since no one can properly devote himself to the service of two masters. Now since it is clear that you have one foot on earth from the fact that you receive with a joyful countenance those who come to you and that you exchange courteous words with them and persuade them to do the works of love, I believe you would do better to enjoy love thoroughly than to lie to God under cloak of some pretense. I believe, however, that God cannot be seriously offended by love, for what is done under the compulsion of nature can be made clean by an easy expiation. Besides, it does not seem at all proper to class as a sin the thing from which the highest good in this life takes its origin and without which no man in the world could be considered worthy of praise.

"I want to explain to you something else that is in my mind, something which I know many keep hidden in their hearts, but which I do not think you are ignorant of, and that is that one kind of love is pure, and one is called mixed. It is the pure love which binds together the hearts of two lovers with feeling of delight. This kind consists in the contemplation of the mind and the affection of the heart; it goes as far as the kiss and the embrace and the modest contact with the nude lover, omitting the final solace, for that is not permitted to those who wish to love purely. This is the kind that anyone who is intent upon love ought to embrace with all his might, for this love goes on increasing without end, and we know that no one ever regretted practicing it, and the more of it one has the more one wants. This love is distinguished by being of such virtue that from it arises all excellence of character, and no injury comes from it, and God sees very little offense in it. No maiden can ever be corrupted by such a love, nor can a widow or a wife receive any harm or suffer any injury to her reputation. This love I cherish, this I follow and ever adore and never cease urgently to demand of you. But that is called mixed love which gets its effect from every delight of the flesh and culminates in the final act of Venus. What sort of love this is you may clearly see from what I have already said, for this kind quickly fails, and one often regrets having practiced it; by it one's neighbor is injured, the Heavenly King is offended, and from it come very grave dangers. But I do not say this as though I meant to condemn mixed love, I merely wish to show which of the two is preferable. But mixed love, too, is real love, and it is praiseworthy, and we say that it is the source of all good things, although from it grave dangers threaten, too. Therefore I approve of both pure love and mixed love, but I prefer to practice pure love. You should therefore put aside all fear of deception and choose one of the two kinds of love."

THE WOMAN SAYS: "From the replies that you have made to me, I know that you have had a great deal of experience in the art of love, so I am asking your opinion upon a certain matter connected with it. Now, since a certain woman of the most excellent character wished to reject one of her two suitors by letting him make his own choice, and to accept the other, she divided the solaces of love in her in this fashion. She said, 'Let one of you choose the upper half of me, and let the other suitor have the lower half.' Without a moment's delay each of them chose his part, and each insisted that he had chosen the better part, and argued that he was more worthy of her love than the other man was because he had chosen the worthier part. Since the woman I have mentioned did not wish to make a hasty decision she asked me, with the consent of the contenders, to give my decision as to which of them should be considered better in what he asked for. I therefore ask you which seems to you to have made the more praiseworthy choice."

THE MAN SAYS: "Since I am asking you for your love and you give me your pretext for not loving, you ought not to consider it discourteous of me if I try in every way to get rid of this excuse that is doing me the harm or to say something that will nullify it. Besides, you know that it will not take anything away from the rights of any lover if Your Prudence chooses to restrain my thoughtless acts. You should therefore be careful to do these things that you ought to do, because I shall never be separated from my determination to love you.

"You ask me, also, to give you my opinion on a matter on which no man of experience should hesitate, for who doubts that the man who chooses the solaces of the upper part should be preferred to the one who seeks the lower? For so far as the solaces of the lower part go, we are in no wise differentiated from brute beasts; but in this respect nature joins us to them. But the solaces of the upper part are, so to speak, attributes peculiar to the nature of man and are by this same nature denied to all the other animals. Therefore the unworthy man who chooses the lower part should be driven out from love just as though he were a dog, and he who chooses the upper part should be accepted as one who honors nature. Besides this, no man has ever been found who was tired of the solaces of the upper part, or satiated by practicing them, but the delight of the lower part quickly palls upon those who practice it, and it makes them repent of what they have done."

CHAPTER VI

The Love of the Clergy

Now, since in the preceding sections we have dealt with three classes of men: namely, commoners, simple nobility, and the higher nobility, and we recall mentioning at the beginning of the discussion the noblest class of all—that is, the clergy—let us speak briefly concerning their love affairs and see where the men of this fourth class get their nobility. Now the clerk is considered to be of the most noble class by virtue of his sacred calling, a nobility which we agree comes from God's bosom and is granted to him by the Divine Will. But so far as this nobility goes, a clerk cannot look for love, for on the strength of it he ought not devote himself to the works of love but is bound to renounce absolutely all the delights of the flesh and to keep himself free from all bodily filth, unspotted for the Lord whose service, according to our belief, he has taken upon him. But since hardly anyone ever lives without carnal sin, and since the life of the clergy is, because of the continual idleness and the great abundance of food, naturally more liable to temptations of the body than that of any other men, if any clerk should wish to enter into the lists of Love let him speak and apply himself to Love's service in accordance with the rank or standing of his parents, as we have already fully explained in regard to the different ranks of men.

CHAPTER VII

The Love of Nuns

Even Love's commandment warns us not to choose for our love any woman whom we may not properly seek to marry. And if anybody should think so little of himself and of both laws as to seek for the love of a nun, he would deserve to be despised by everybody and he ought to be avoided as an abominable beast.

CHAPTER VIII

The Easy Attainment of One's Object

The readiness to grant requests is, we say, the same thing in women as overvoluptuousness in men—a thing which all agree should be a total stranger in the court of Love. For he who is so tormented by carnal passion that he cannot embrace anyone in heartfelt love, but basely lusts after every woman he sees, is not called a lover but a counterfeiter of love and a pretender, and he is lower than a shameless dog. Indeed the man who is so wanton that he cannot confine himself to the love of one woman deserves to be considered an impetuous ass. It will therefore be clear to you that you are bound to avoid an overabundance of passion and that you ought not to seek the love of a woman who you know will grant easily what you seek.

CHAPTER IX

The Love of Peasants

If you should, by some chance, fall in love with a peasant woman, be careful to puff her up with lots of praise and then, when you find a convenient place, do not hesitate to take what you seek and to embrace her by force. For you can hardly soften their outward inflexibility so far that they will grant you their embraces quietly or permit you to have the solaces you desire unless first you use a little compulsion as a convenient cure for their shyness. We do not say these things, however, because we want to persuade you to love such women, but only so that, if through lack of caution you should be driven to love them, you may know, in brief compass, what to do.

BOOK TWO

How Love May Be Retained

CHAPTER I

How Love, When It Has Been Acquired, May Be Kept

Now since we have already said enough about acquiring love, it is not unfitting that we should next see and describe how this love may be retained after it has once been acquired. The man who wants to keep his love affair for a long time untroubled should above all things be careful not to let it be known to any outsider, but should keep it hidden from everybody; because when a number of people begin to get wind of such an affair, it ceases to develop naturally and even loses what progress it has already made. Furthermore a lover ought to appear to his beloved wise in every respect and restrained in his conduct, and he should do nothing disagreeable that might annoy her. And if inadvertently he should do something improper that offends her, let him straightway confess with downcast face that he has done wrong, and let him give the excuse that he lost his temper or make some other suitable explanation that will fit the case. And every man ought to be sparing of praise of his beloved when he is among other men; he should not spend a great deal of time in places where she is. When he is with other men, if he meets her in a group of women, he should not try to communicate with her by signs, but should treat her almost like a stranger lest some person spying on their love might have opportunity to spread malicious gossip. Lovers should not even nod to each other unless they are sure that nobody is watching them. Every man

25

should also wear things that his beloved likes and pay a reasonable amount of attention to his appearance—not too much because excessive care for one's looks is distasteful to everybody and leads people to despise the good looks that one has. If the lover is lavish in giving, that helps him retain a love he has acquired, for all lovers ought to despise all worldly riches and should give alms to those who have need of them. Also, if the lover is one who is fitted to be a warrior, he should see to it that his courage is apparent to everybody, for it detracts very much from the good character of a man if he is timid in a fight. A lover should always offer his services and obedience freely to every lady, and he ought to root out all his pride and be very humble. Then, too, he must keep in mind the general rule that lovers must not neglect anything that good manners demand or good breeding suggests, but they should be very careful to do everything of this sort. Love may also be retained by indulging in the sweet and delightful solaces of the flesh, but only in such manner and in such number that they may never seem wearisome to the loved one. Let the lover strive to practice gracefully and manfully any act or mannerism which he has noticed is pleasing to his beloved. A clerk should not, of course, affect the manners or the dress of the laity, for no one is likely to please his beloved, if she is a wise woman, by wearing strange clothing or by practicing manners that do not suit his status. Furthermore a lover should make every attempt to be constantly in the company of good men and to avoid completely the society of the wicked. For association with the vulgar makes a lover who joins them a thing of contempt to his beloved.

CHAPTER II

How Love, Once Consummated, May Be Increased

We shall attempt to show you in a few words how love may be increased after it has been consummated. Now in the first place it is said to increase if the lovers see each other rarely and with difficulty; for the greater the difficulty of exchanging solaces, the more do the desire for them and the feeling of love increase. Love increases, too, if one of the lovers shows that he is angry at the other; for the lover falls at once into a great fear that this feeling which has arisen in his beloved may last forever. Love increases, likewise, if one of the lovers feels real jealousy, which is called, in fact, the nurse of love. Even if he does not suffer from real jealousy, but from a shameful suspicion, still by virtue of this his love always increases and grows more powerful. Love increases, too, if it happens to last after it has been made public; ordinarily it does not last, but begins to fail just as soon as it is revealed. Again, if one of the lovers dreams about the other, that gives rise to love, or if love already exists it increases it. So, too, if you know that someone is trying to win your beloved away from you, that will no doubt increase your love and you will begin to feel more affection for her. I will go further and say that even though you know perfectly well that some other man is enjoying the embraces of your beloved, this will make you begin to value her solaces all the more, unless your greatness of soul and nobility of mind keep you from such wickedness. When you have gone to some other place or are about to go away—that increases your love, and so do the scoldings and beatings that lovers suffer from their parents, for not only does a scolding lecture cause love to increase after it is perfected, but it even gives a perfect reason for beginning a love affair that has not yet started. Frequent dwelling with delight on the thought of the beloved is of value in increasing love; so is the sight of her eyes when you are by yourselves and fearful, and her eager acceptance of a demand for the acts of love. Love is greatly intensified by a carriage and a way of walking that please the beloved, by a readiness to say pretty things, by a pleasant manner of speaking, and by hearing men sing the praises of the loved one.

CHAPTER III

In What Ways Love May Be Decreased

Now let us see in what ways love may be decreased. Too many opportunities for exchanging solaces, too many opportunities of seeing the loved one, too much chance to talk to each other all decrease love, and so does an uncultured appearance or manner of walking on the part of the lover or the sudden loss of his property. Love decreases, too, if the woman finds that her lover is foolish and indiscreet, or if he seems to go beyond reasonable bounds in his demands for love, or if she sees that he has no regard for her modesty and will not forgive her bashfulness. Love decreases, too, if the woman considers that her lover is cowardly in battle, or sees that he is unrestrained in his speech or spoiled by the vice of arrogance.

Other things which weaken love are blasphemy against God or His saints, mockery of the ceremonies of the Church, and a deliberate withholding of charity from the poor. We find that love decreases very sharply if one is unfaithful to his friend, or if he brazenly says one thing while he deceitfully conceals a different idea in his heart. Love decreases, too, if the lover piles up more wealth than is proper, or if he is too ready to go to law over trifles.

CHAPTER IV

How Love May Come to an End

Now having treated briefly of the lessening of love we shall try next to add for you an explanation of how it may come to an end. First of all we see that love comes to an end if one of the lovers breaks faith or tries to break faith with the other, or if he is found to go astray from the Catholic religion. It comes to an end also after it has been openly revealed and made known to men. So, too, if one of the lovers has plenty of money and does not come to the aid of the other who is in great need and lacks a great many things, then love usually becomes very cheap and comes to an ignominious end. An old love also ends when a new one begins, because no one can love two people at the same time. Furthermore, inequality of love and a fraudulent and deceitful duplicity of heart always drive out love, for a deceitful lover, no matter how worthy he is otherwise, ought to be rejected by any woman. Again, if by some chance one of the lovers becomes incapable of carrying out love's duties, love can no longer last between them and deserts them and deserts them completely. Likewise if one of the lovers becomes insane or develops a sudden timidity, love flees and becomes hateful.

You may, however, ask whether a love once ended can ever come to life again. If this failure of love comes from ignorance of some particular thing, there is no doubt but that it may be revived; however, where it grows out of some misdeed of the lover or of some defect in his nature, we cannot remember any case where it has revived, although we do not say that it cannot, except perhaps in cases where this failure is due to some defect in the lover's nature. And if love should at some time happen to come to life again, we do not think that the lovers would have perfect confidence in each other.

CHAPTER V

Indications That One's Love Is Returned

Now that we have thus disposed of these questions and have, in a short space, finished them up, let us add to them a discussion of how to find out whether one's love is returned. There are many ways in which a lover can find out the faith of his beloved and test her feelings. If you see that your loved one is missing all sorts of opportunities to meet you or is putting false obstacles in your path, you cannot hope long to enjoy her love. So, too, if you find her, for no reason at all, growing half-hearted about giving you the usual solaces, you may see that her faith is wavering. If you find that she keeps out of your sight more than she was accustomed to do, her feelings are not very stable; and if she tries to hide from your faithful messenger, there is no doubt that she has turned you adrift in the mighty waves and that her love for you is only feigned. If at the very moment of delight when she is offering you her sweet solaces the act is more wearisome to her than usual, you need not doubt that she has no love for you. So, too, if she finds more fault with you than usual or demands things that she has not been in the habit of demanding, you may know that your love will not last much longer. Again, if when she is with you or someone else she frequently talks about what you did and what the other man did, without making any distinction between you, or if on some clever pretext she asks what sort of man he is or what sort of character he has, you may know that she is thinking about the love of the other man. Moreover, if you find that she is paying more attention to the care of her person than she had been doing, either her love for you is growing or she is interested in the love of someone else.

CHAPTER VI

If One of the Lovers Is Unfaithful to the Other

If one of the lovers should be unfaithful to the other, and the offender is the man, and he has an eye to a new love affair, he renders himself wholly unworthy of his former love, and she ought to deprive him completely of her embraces.

But what if he should be unfaithful to his beloved,—not with the idea of finding a new love, but because he has been driven to it by an irresistible passion for another woman? What, for instance, if chance should present to him an unknown woman in a convenient place or what if at a time when Venus is urging him on to that which I am talking about he should meet with a little strumpet or somebody's servant girl? Should he, just because he played with her in the grass, lose the love of his beloved? We can say without fear of contradiction that just for this a lover is not considered unworthy of the love of his beloved unless he indulges in so many excesses with a number of women that we may conclude that he is overpassionate. But if whenever he becomes acquainted with a woman he pesters her to gain his end, or if he attains his object as a result of his efforts, then rightly he does deserve to be deprived of his former love, because there is strong presumption that he has acted in this way with an eye toward a new one, especially where he has strayed with a woman of the nobility or otherwise of an honorable estate.

I know that once when I sought advice I got the answer that a true lover can never desire a new love unless he knows that for some definite and sufficient reason the old love is dead; we know from our own experience that this rule is very true. We have fallen in love with a woman of the most admirable character, although we have never had, or hope to have, any fruit of this love. For we are compelled to pine away for love of a woman of such lofty station that we dare not say one word about it, nor dare we throw ourself upon her mercy, and so at length we are forced to find our body shipwrecked. But although rashly and without foresight we have fallen into such great waves in this tempest, still we cannot think about a new love or look for any other way to free ourself.

But since you are making a special study of the subject of love, you may well ask whether a man can have a pure love for one woman and a mixed or common love with another. We will show you, by an unanswerable argument, that no one can feel affection for two women in this fashion. For although pure love and mixed love may seem to be very different things, if you will look at the matter properly you will see that pure love, so far as its substance goes, is the same as mixed love and comes from the same feeling of the heart. The substance of the love is the same in each case, and only the manner and form of loving are different, as this illustration will make clear to you. Sometimes we see a man with a desire to drink his wine unmixed, and at another time his appetite prompts him to drink only water or wine and water mixed; although his appetite manifests itself differently, the substance of it is the same and unchanged. So likewise when two people have long been united by pure love and afterwards desire to practice mixed love, the substance of the love remains the same in them, although the manner and form and the way of practicing it are different.

CHAPTER VII

Various Decisions in Love Cases

Now then, let us come to various decisions in cases of love:

I. A certain knight loved his lady beyond all measure and enjoyed her full embrace, but she did not love him with equal ardor. He sought to leave her, but she, desiring to retain him in his former status, opposed his wish. In this affair the Countess of Champagne gave this response: "It is considered very unseemly for a woman to seek to be loved and yet to refuse to love. It is silly for anybody disrespectfully to ask of others what she herself wholly refuses to give to others."

II. A certain man asked the Lady Ermengarde of Narbonne to make clear where there was the greater affection—between lovers or between married people. The lady gave him a logical answer. She said: "We consider that marital affection and the true love of lovers are wholly different and arise from entirely different sources, and so the ambiguous nature of the word prevents the comparison of the things and we have to place them in different classes. Comparisons of more or less are not valid when things are grouped together under an ambiguous heading and the comparison is made in regard to that ambiguous term. It is no true comparison to say that a name is simpler than a body or that the outline of a speech is better arranged than the delivery."

III. The same man asked the same lady this question. A certain woman had been married, but was now separated from her husband by a divorce, and her former husband sought eagerly for her love. In this case the lady replied: "If any two people have been married and afterwards separate in any way, we consider love between them wholly wicked."

IV. A certain knight was in love with a woman who had given her love to another man, but he got from her this much hope of her love—that if it should ever happen that she lost the love of her beloved, then without a doubt her love would go to this man. A little while after this the woman married her lover. The other knight then demanded that she give him the fruit of the hope she had granted him, but this she absolutely refused to do, saying that she had not lost the love of her lover. In this affair the Queen gave her decision as follows: "We dare not oppose the opinion of the Countess of Champagne, who ruled that love can exert no power between husband and wife. Therefore we recommend that the lady should grant the love she has promised."

V. The Queen was also asked which was preferable: the love of a young man or of one advanced in years. She answered this question with wonderful subtlety by saying, "We distinguish between a good and a better love by the man's knowledge and his character and his praiseworthy manners, not by his age. But as regards that natural instinct of passion, young men are usually more eager to gratify it with older women than with young ones of their own age; those who are older prefer to receive the embraces and kisses of young women rather than of the older ones. But on the other hand a woman whether young or somewhat older likes the embraces and solaces of young men better than those of older ones. The explanation of this fact seems to be a physiological one."

CHAPTER VIII

The Rules of Love

Let us come now to the rules of love, and I shall try to present to you very briefly those rules which the King of Love is said to have proclaimed with his own mouth and to have given in writing to all lovers.

One of the knights of Britain was riding alone through the royal forest, going to see Arthur, and when he got well into the interior of this forest he came unexpectedly upon a young girl of marvellous beauty, sitting on a fine horse and binding up her hair. The knight lost no time in saluting her, and she answered him courteously and said, "Briton, no matter how hard you try you can't succeed in your quest unless you have our help." When he had heard these words he quickly asked the girl to tell him what he had come for, and then after that he would believe what she said to him. The young girl said to him, "When you asked for the love of a certain British lady, she told you that you could never obtain it unless you first brought back that victorious hawk which, men say, is on a golden perch in Arthur's court." The Briton admitted that all this was true, and the girl went on, "You can't get this hawk that you are seeking unless you prove, by a combat in Arthur's palace, that you enjoy the love of a more beautiful lady than any man at Arthur's court has; you can't even enter the palace until you show the guards the hawk's gauntlet, and you can't get this gauntlet except by overcoming two mighty knights in a double combat."

The Briton answered, "I know that I cannot accomplish this task without your aid, and so I will submit myself to your direction, humbly beseeching you to give me your help in the matter and to permit me to claim, in view of the fact that you are directing me, that I enjoy the love of the more beautiful lady."

The young girl said to him, "If your heart is so stout that you are not afraid to carry out those things of which we have spoken, you may have from us what you ask." The Briton answered, "If you will grant my request, I know that I shall succeed in all that I hope for."

The young girl said to him, "Then let what you request be freely granted to you." Then she gave him the kiss of love and said, indicating the horse on which she was sitting, "This horse will take you everywhere you want to go; but

you must go forward without any fear and oppose with the
highest courage all those who try to stop you. But bear in
mind that after you have gained the victory over the first
two who defend the gauntlet you must not accept it from
them, but must take it for yourself from the golden pillar
where it hangs; otherwise you cannot prevail in the combat
at the palace or accomplish what you desire."

When she finished speaking, the Briton put on his arms
and, after she had given him leave to depart, began to go
at a walk through the wood. At length, as he was passing
through a wild and lonely place, he came to a certain river
of marvellous breadth and depth, with great waves in it,
and because of the great height of its banks it was impossible
for anyone to reach it. But as he rode along the edge of the
bank he came to a bridge which was of gold and had one
end fastened to each bank; the middle of it, however, rested
in the water, and he could see that it was so shaken that
great waves often covered it. At that end of it which the
Briton was approaching there was a knight of a ferocious
aspect who was sitting on a horse. The Briton greeted him
courteously enough, but the knight scorned to return the
greeting and said, "Armed Briton, who come from such
distant regions, what are you seeking?"

The Briton answered, "I am trying to cross the river by
the bridge;" and the bridge keeper said, "Then you must
be seeking death, which no stranger here has been able to
escape. But if you want to go back home and leave all your
arms here, I will take pity on your youth which has led you
so rashly and so foolishly into other men's countries and into
strange realms."

The Briton replied, "If I were to lay down my arms,
you would gain little credit for the victory of a man in arms
over an unarmed man; but if you can keep an armed man
from going along the public way, then you may consider that
your victory has won you glory. If you do not make way
peaceably for me to go across the bridge, I shall simply try
to force a passage with my sword."

When the bridge keeper heard that the young man was trying to force a passage with his sword, he began to gnash his teeth, and he fell into a great rage and said, "Young man, Britain sent you here in an evil hour, since you shall perish by the sword in this wilderness, and you will never be able to bring back news of the country to your lady. Woe to you, wretched Briton, who have not been afraid to seek the place of your death at the persuasion of a woman!" Then spurring his horse against the Briton he began to attack him with his sharp sword and to hammer him so cruelly that one stroke, glancing off his shield, cut through two folds of his hauberk and into the flesh of his side so that the blood commenced to flow in abundance from the wound. The young man, stung by the pain of his wound, directed the point of his lance at the knight of the bridge, and with a mighty thrust pierced him through, bore him from his horse, and stretched him shamefully upon the ground. But when the Briton was about to smite off his head, the bridge keeper, by the most humble entreaties, sought and obtained mercy.

But on the other side of the river there stood a man of tremendous size, who seeing the bridge keeper overcome by the Briton and this same Briton starting to cross the golden bridge, began to shake it so violently that much of the time it was hidden by the waves. But the Briton, having great confidence in the excellence of his horse, did not cease to press forward manfully over the bridge and at length, after great difficulty and many duckings, he arrived at the farther end of it by virtue of his horse's efforts; there he drowned beneath the water the man who had been shaking the bridge and bound up the wound in his own side as well as he could.

After this the Briton began to ride through very beautiful fields and after he had ridden for about a mile the path came out into a pleasant meadow, fragrant with all sorts of flowers. In this meadow was a palace, marvellously built in a circular form and very beautifully decorated. He could not find a door anywhere in the palace, nor could he see any inhabitants; but in the fields he found silver tables, and on them were all sorts of food and drink set among snow-white napkins. In the same pleasant meadow was a shell of the purest silver in which there was sufficient food and drink for a horse. He therefore drove his horse off to feed, and he himself walked completely around the palace; but finding no sign of any entrance to the dwelling or any evidence that the place was inhabited, he drew near to the table and, driven by his hunger, began ravenously to devour the food he found there. A very little while after he had begun to eat, a door of the palace opened quickly with such violence that the shock of it resounded like near-by thunder, and suddenly out of this door came a man of gigantic size, brandishing in his hands a copper club of immense weight which he shook like a straw without the least effort. To the youth at the table he said, "What sort of man are you, so presumptuous that you were not afraid to come to this royal place and so coolly and disrespectfully to eat the food on the royal table of the knights?"

The Briton answered, "The royal table should be freely open to everybody, and it is not proper that anybody should be refused the royal food and drink. Moreover it is right for me to partake of the rations prepared for the knights, since knighthood is my sole care and a knightly task has brought me to this place. You are therefore doubly discourteous in trying to forbid me the royal table."

To this the doorkeeper replied, "Although this is the royal table, it is not proper for anyone to eat at it except those who are assigned to this palace, and they allow no one to go beyond this point unless he fights with the palace guards and defeats them. And if anyone is beaten by them, there is no hope for him. Therefore get up from the table and hurry back to where you belong, or tell me that you want to fight your way onward and why you have come this far."

The Briton said to him, "I am seeking the hawk's gauntlet; that is why I came. When I get it I shall try to go further and as victor in Arthur's court take the hawk. Where is this palace guard you mention who will keep me from going on?"

The doorkeeper replied, "You fool! What madness possesses you, Briton! It would be easier for you to die and come to life again ten times than to get those things you mention. I am the palace guard who will deprive you of your reputation and spoil Britain of your youth. I am so strong that when I am angry two hundred of the best knights of Britain can hardly withstand me."

The Briton answered, "Although you say you are very powerful, I would like to fight with you to show you what sort of men Britain produces; however, it isn't proper for a knight to fight with a footman."

The doorkeeper said to him, "I see that your bad luck has brought you to death in this place where my right hand has felled more than a thousand. And although I am not reckoned among the knights, I would like to fight with you while you are on horseback, because then if you yield to the valor of a footman you will have good reason to know what sort of person would be overcome by the boldness of a man like me if I were on horseback."

To this the Briton answered, "God forbid that I should ever fight on horseback against a man on foot, for against a foot soldier every man should fight on foot," and grasping his arms he rushed bravely at the enemy before him and with a blow of his sword slightly damaged the latter's shield. The guardian of the palace, greatly enraged at this and contemptuous of the Britain's small size, shook his brazen club so furiously that the Briton's shield was almost shattered by the concussion, and he himself was greatly terrified. Thinking that a second blow would finish the Briton, the guard raised his hand to strike again, but before the blow could fall the other quickly feinted and with his sword caught him on the arm, so that the right hand, still holding the club, fell to the ground. But as he was about to put an end to him, the guard cried out, "Are you the one discourteous knight that sweet Britain has produced, you who would slay a wounded man? If you will spare my life I can easily get for you what you want, but without me you can gain nothing."

The Briton said, "Porter, I will spare your life if you will do what you promise."

The guard said, "Wait a bit and I will quickly get you the hawk's gauntlet."

The Briton answered, "You robber and deceiver of man! Now I see plainly that you are trying to cheat me. If you want to save your life just show me the place where that gauntlet of yours is kept."

The guard then led the Briton into the innermost part of the palace where there was a very beautiful golden column that held up the whole weight of the palace, and on this column hung the gauntlet he was seeking. As he grasped it boldly and held it firmly in his left hand he heard a great noise, and although he saw nobody, a wailing began to resound throughout the palace, and a cry, "Woe! woe! in spite of us the victor enemy is carrying away the spoil."

He left the palace and, mounting his horse which was already saddled, continued his journey until he came to a delightful place where there were more of those beautiful fields filled with flowers, and in the fields was a palace finely built of gold. Its length was six hundred cubits, and its width two hundred. The roof and all the outer walls were of silver, and the inside was all of gold set with precious stones. The palace was divided into a great many rooms, and in the hall of state King Arthur was sitting on a golden throne surrounded by beautiful women, more than I could count, and before him stood many splendid knights. In this palace was a beautifully fashioned golden perch on which was the hawk he was seeking, and chained near by lay two hawking dogs. But before he could get to the palace his way was blocked by a heavily fortified barbican, raised to protect the palace, and to the defense of it were assigned twelve very strong knights who permitted no one to pass unless he showed them the gauntlet for the hawk or forced his way sword in hand.

When the Briton saw them, he quickly showed them the gauntlet and they fell back saying, "Your life isn't safe if you go on this way; it will lead you to great trouble." But the Briton continued on to the interior of the palace and saluted King Arthur. When the knights pressed him to know why he had come here, he replied that he had come to carry off the hawk. One of the knights of the court asked him, "Why are you trying to get the hawk?" and he replied, "Because I enjoy the love of a more beautiful woman than any knight in this court has." The other answered him, "Before you can take away the hawk you will have to fight to prove that statement." "Gladly!" said the Briton. After a suitable shield had been given him both took their places armed within the lists; setting spurs to their horses, they rushed together violently, shattering each other's shields and splintering their lances; then with their swords they smote each other and hewed to pieces the iron armor. After they had fought in this fashion for a long time, the vision of the knight of the palace, whom the Briton had struck on the head with two shrewd blows in rapid succession, began to be so disturbed that he could see almost nothing. When the Briton perceived this, he leapt boldly upon him and quickly struck him from his horse. Then he seized the hawk, and, glancing as he did so at the two dogs, he saw a written parchment, which was fastened to the perch with a little gold chain. When he inquired carefully concerning this, he was told, "This is the parchment on which are written the rules of love which the King of Love himself, with his own mouth, pronounced for lovers. You should take it with you and make these rules known to lovers if you want to take away the hawk peaceably."

He took the parchment, and after he had been given courteous permission to depart, quickly returned, without any opposition, to the lady of the wood, whom he found in the same place in the grove where she was when he first came upon her as he was riding along. She rejoiced greatly over the victory he had gained and dismissed him with these words, "Dearest friend, go with my permission, since sweet Britain desires you. But, that your departure may not seem too grievous to you, I ask you to come here sometimes alone, and you can always have me with you." He kissed her thirteen times over and went joyfully back to Britain. Afterwards he looked over the rules which he had found written in the parchment, and then, in accordance with the answer he had previously received, he made them known to all lovers. These are the rules.

     I. Marriage is no real excuse for not loving.

    II. He who is not jealous cannot love.

    III. No one can be bound by a double love.

    IV. It is well known that love is always increasing or decreasing.

    V. That which a lover takes against his will of his beloved has no relish.

    VI. Boys do not love until they arrive at the age of maturity.

    VII. When one lover dies, a widowhood of two years is required of the survivor.

    VIII. No one should be deprived of love without the very best of reasons.

    IX. No one can love unless he is impelled by the persuasion of love.

    X. Love is always a stranger in the home of avarice.

    XI. It is not proper to love any woman whom one should be ashamed to seek to marry.

    XII. A true lover does not desire to embrace in love anyone except his beloved.

    XIII. When made public love rarely endures.

    XIV. The easy attainment of love makes it of little value; difficulty of attainment makes it prized.

    XV. Every lover regularly turns pale in the presence of his beloved.

    XVI. When a lover suddenly catches sight of his beloved his heart palpitates.

XVII. A new love puts to flight an old one.

XVIII. Good character alone makes any man worthy of love.

XIX. If love diminishes, it quickly fails and rarely revives.

XX. A man in love is always apprehensive.

XXI. Real jealousy always increases the feeling of love.

XXII. Jealousy, and therefore love, are increased when one suspects his beloved.

XXIII. He whom the thought of love vexes, eats and sleeps very little.

XXIV. Every act of a lover ends in the thought of his beloved.

XXV. A true lover considers nothing good except what he thinks will please his beloved.

XXVI. Love can deny nothing to love.

XXVII. A lover can never have enough of the solaces of his beloved.

XXVIII. A slight presumption causes a lover to suspect his beloved.

XXIX. A man who is vexed by too much passion usually does not love.

XXX. A true lover is constantly and without intermission possessed by the thought of his beloved.

XXXI. Nothing forbids one woman being loved by two men or one man by two women.

BOOK THREE

The Rejection of Love

Now, friend Walter, if you will lend attentive ears to those things which after careful consideration we wrote down for you because you urged us so strongly, you can lack nothing in the art of love since in this little book we gave you the theory of the subject fully and completely, being willing to accede to your requests because of the great love we have for you. You should know that we did not do this because we consider it advisable for you or any other man to fall in love, but for fear lest you might think us stupid; we believe, though, that any man who devotes his efforts to love loses all his usefulness. Read this little book, then, not as one seeking to take up the life of a lover, but that, invigorated by the theory and trained to excite the minds of women to love, you may, by refraining from so doing, win an eternal recompense and thereby deserve a greater reward from God. For God is more pleased with a man who is able to sin and does not, than with a man who has no opportunity to sin.

Now for many reasons any wise man is bound to avoid all the deeds of love and to oppose all its mandates. The first of these reasons is one which it is not right for anyone to oppose, for no man, so long as he devotes himself to the service of love, can please God by any other works, even if they are good ones. For God hates, and in both testaments commands the punishment of, those whom he sees engaged in the works of Venus outside the bonds of wedlock or caught in the toils of any sort of passion. What good therefore can be found in a thing in which nothing is done except what is contrary to the will of God? Indeed for a mortal man we consider it a very great disgrace and an offense against Almighty God if by following the enticements of the flesh and the pleasures of the body he slips back again into the snares of Hell, from which the Heavenly Father Himself once redeemed him by shedding the blood of His Only-Begotten Son.

Chastity and the restraining of carnal desires are reckoned among the virtues, and so their opposites, lust and the delight of the flesh, must necessarily be reckoned among the vices. Therefore every man must flee from them, because there is nothing that men more desire while they live on earth than to have a praiseworthy name among their fellows and to have their reputation spread widely throughout the world. But nobody can keep his reputation bright and unharmed or have a good name among men unless he is adorned with the virtues. And no one can have the adornment of the virtues if he is spotted with the tiniest black speck of vice, for virtue and vice "do not go well together or dwell in the same abode."

It is not considered to a woman's credit either if she begins to devote herself to the employments of love, even if she is loved by one of royal race. Indeed although in men an excess of love or of lechery is tolerated on account of the boldness of the sex, in women it is considered a damnable offense; a woman's good name is ruined by it, and every wise person looks upon her as an unclean harlot and holds her in utter contempt.

But still another argument seems very much opposed to love. Many evils come from love, but I do not see that anything that is good for men comes from it; that delight of the flesh which we embrace with such great eagerness is not in the nature of a good, but rather, as men agree, it is a damnable sin which even in married persons is scarcely to be classed among the venial faults which are not sins, according to the word of the prophet, who said, "For behold I was conceived in iniquities and in sins did my mother conceive me." (Ps. 50,7)

Besides this we know beyond a doubt that God Himself

is the fountain head and origin of chastity and of modesty, and from Scripture we know that the Devil is really the author of love and lechery. And so, because of their sources, we are bound forever to observe modesty and chastity and to shun lechery completely, because we agree that that which the Devil has given rise to cannot be at all wholesome for men or give them anything that we can praise. But that which God gives rise to can by no means result in anything that is bad for men or prove evil for them. You ought to know, then, what mental blindness a man suffers who leaves God's services and busies himself with that of the Devil. For the Devil promises to his soldiers many things, and pleasant ones, too, but afterwards he pays them with very bitter ones; he always does the opposite of what he has promised, since he has been a liar from the beginning and he stood not in the truth. He is indeed in the habit of giving his servants a wretched retribution, for the more they serve him the greater are the torments that they deserve to earn from him and the greater the tortures they deserve to suffer. But God is not like this; in place of the good and pleasant things He has promised us, He gives us very much better and very much sweeter ones; because He is the Way, the Truth, and the Life and so with good reason He pays us more richly than He has promised to. Whoever will with full confidence entrust himself in His company will never fall into the toils of any enemy, but will be led safely to his desired goal and to eternal glory. With good reason, therefore, every man is bound to reject love and deeds of wantonness and to strive for complete bodily chastity.

Many are the evils of love. Love wickedly breaks up marriage and without reason turns a husband from his wife, whom God, in the law He gave us, firmly bade not to separate from her husband. With a wife we overcome our passion without sinning, and we do away with the incentives to wantonness without staining our souls; and we have by our wives legitimate offspring who will worthily comfort us both living and dying, and in them God can see that we bear Him worthy fruit. But even if at times a man does get offspring through fornication, such a son can be of no comfort to his father, since he cannot even inherit from him. Indeed, the Scriptures tell us that sons born of fornication are the shame of their parent, and we do not think that they are acceptable to God; Holy Scripture seems to make this clear to us when it says, "The sons of adulterers are abominable to God."

Since then, all sorts of wickedness come from love and nothing good can be found to spring from it, but only untold torments for mankind—why, O foolish young man, do you seek to love and to deprive yourself of the grace of God and of your everlasting heritage? We hope that your noble birth and excellence of character may never be spotted by the infection of Venus or stained by illicit commerce with a woman or soiled with her filthiness, for there is nothing in the world more loathsome or more wearisome than to meditate too intently on the nature or the characteristics of a woman.

If a man proves to be chaste and generous, he is not easily harmed by the detractions of anyone else or deprived of the praise that is due him. You will be wise, therefore, if you make great efforts to attain that which adorns all the good qualities that are to be found in a man, and has the power to cover up many excesses in anyone. Do not be surprised that I said "chaste" and added "and generous," for without generosity all virtue in a man seems to lie dead and to bear no fruit of praise according to the word of the Apostle James, who said, "All faith without works is dead." So, too, all virtue without generosity is considered nothing.

Another argument, too, seems clearly to oppose lovers. By love and the work of Venus men's bodies are weakened, and so they are made less powerful in warfare. By love men are weakened in three very logical ways: by the mere act of Venus, as the physiologists tell us, the powers of the body are very much lessened; love causes one to eat less and drink less, and so not unreasonably the body, being less nourished, has less strength; finally, love takes away a man's sleep and deprives him of all rest. But lack of sleep is followed in a man by bad digestion and great weakening of the body. In a fourth way, too, it may not unfittingly be said that the human body is weakened, for we believe that through sin all of God's gifts in a man are lessened and the span of man's life is shortened. Since, therefore, bodily strength is a great and especial gift to man, you will do wrong if you strive after things which can for any reason cause this particular gift to fail in you or to be in any way decreased.

For yet another reason I urge you not to love: that is because in a wise man wisdom loses its function if he loves. No matter how full of wisdom any man may be, if he is seduced to the work of Venus he cannot be moderate or restrain by his wisdom the impulse of wantonness or keep from doing the things that lead to death. Who was filled with greater wisdom than Solomon, yet he sinned by wantoning beyond measure and because of his love for women he did not fear to worship strange gods. What lover of women, then, can moderate his own desire if men so strong in the precepts of wisdom could make no use of it when the love of women was in question, and could not restrain their wantonness?

Again we confound lovers with another argument. The mutual love which you seek in women you cannot find, for no woman ever loved a man or could bind herself to a lover in the mutual bonds of love. For a woman's desire is to get rich through love, but not to give her lover the solaces that please him. Even though you have given a woman innumerable presents, if she discovers that you are less attentive about giving her things than you used to be, or if she learns that you have lost your money, she will treat you like a perfect stranger who has come from some other country, and everything you do will bore her or annoy her.

Woman is also a miser, because there isn't a wickedness in the world that men can think of that she will not boldly indulge in for the sake of money, and, even if she has an abundance she will not help anyone who is in need. You can more easily scratch a diamond with your fingernail than you can by any human ingenuity get a woman to consent to giving you any of her savings. Just as Epicurus believed that the highest good lay in serving the belly, so a woman thinks that the only things worth while in this world are riches and holding on to what she has.

That every woman is envious is also found to be a general rule because a woman is always consumed with jealousy over another woman's beauty, and she loses all pleasure in what she has. Even if she knows that it is the beauty of her own daughter that is being praised she can hardly avoid being tortured by hidden envy.

And so it naturally follows that a woman is a slanderer, because only slander can spring from envy and hate. It is not easy to find a woman whose tongue can ever spare anybody or who can keep from words of detraction. Every woman thinks that by running down others she adds to her own praise and increases her own reputation—a fact which shows very clearly to everybody that women have very little sense.

Woman is also such a slave to her belly that there is nothing she would be ashamed to assent to if she were assured of a fine meal, and no matter how much she has she never has any hope that she can satisfy her appetite when she is hungry; she never invites anybody to eat with her, but when she eats she always seeks out hidden and retired places and she usually likes to eat more than normal. We can detect all these qualities in Eve, the first woman, who although she was created by the hand of God without man's agency was not afraid to eat the forbidden fruit and for her gluttony was deservedly driven from her home in Paradise. So if that woman who was created by the hand of God without sin could not refrain from the vice of gluttony, what about the others whom their mothers conceived in sin and who never live free from fault? Therefore let it be laid down for you as a general rule that you will rarely fail to get from a woman anything you desire if you will take the trouble to feed her lavishly and often.

Woman is commonly found to be fickle, too, because no woman ever makes up her mind so firmly on any subject that she will not quickly change it on a little persuading from anyone. A woman is just like melting wax, which is always ready to take a new form and to receive the impress of anybody's seal. No woman can make you such a firm promise that she will not change her mind about the matter in a few minutes. No woman is ever of the same mind for an hour at a time.

We know that everything a woman says is said with the intention of deceiving, because she always has one thing in her heart and another on her lips. No woman ever trusts any of her men friends, and she thinks every one of them is a downright deceiver; so she always keeps herself in the mood for deception, and everything she says is deceitful and uttered with a mental reservation. Therefore never rely upon a woman's promise or upon her oath, because there is no honesty in her; always be careful to keep your intentions hidden from her, and never tell her your secrets; in that way you may cheat one trick with another and forestall her frauds.

Every woman is likewise stained by the sin of disobedience, because there isn't in the world a woman so wise and discreet that, if anyone forbids her to misuse anything she will not strive against this prohibition with all her might and do what she is told not to. Wasn't it Eve, the first woman, who, although she was formed by the hand of God, destroyed herself by the sin of disobedience and lost the glory of immortality and by her offense brought all her descendants to the destruction of death? Therefore if you want a woman to do anything, you can get her to do it by ordering her to do the opposite.

Vainglory also mightily possesses woman, since you cannot find a woman in the world who does not delight in the praise of men above everything else and who does not think that every word spoken about her has to do with her praise. This fault can be seen even in Eve, the first woman, who ate the forbidden food in order to have knowledge of good and evil. Furthermore, you cannot find a woman so lowly-born that she will not tell you she has famous relatives and is descended from a family of great men and who will not make all sorts of boasts about herself.

You will find, too, that every woman is a liar, because there isn't a woman living who doesn't make up things that are untrue and who dosen't boldly declare what is false. Even for a trifle a woman will swear falsely a thousand times, and for a tiny gain she will make up innumerable lies.

Again, every woman is a drunkard, that is, she likes to drink wine. There is no woman who would blush to drink excellent Falernian wine with a hundred gossips in one day, nor will she be so refreshed by that many drinks of un-diluted wine that she will refuse another if it is brought her.

Every woman is also loud-mouthed, since no one of them can keep her tongue from abuses, and if she loses a single egg she will keep up a clamor all day like a barking dog, and she will disturb the whole neighborhood over a trifle. We even see many women who are so anxious to talk that when they are alone they talk to themselves and speak out loud. A woman will boldly contradict everything you say, and she can never agree with anything, but she always tries to give her opinion on every subject.

Indeed, a woman does not love a man with her whole heart, because there is not one of them who keeps faith with her husband or her lover; when another man comes along, you will find that her faithfulness wavers. It doesn't seem proper, therefore, for any prudent man to fall in love with any woman, because she never keeps faith with any man; everybody knows that she ought to be spurned for the in-numerable weighty reasons that have already been given.

Besides this there is another reason why Love seems very hateful, and this is that he very often carries unequal weights and always makes a man fall in love with some woman whom he cannot by any amount of solicitation obtain, since she does not return his love, not having been wounded by Cupid's arrow. Therefore you should not choose to commit yourself to him who compels you to seek with all your might something which he himself arranges shall be utterly denied you. If Love wanted to be considered a just ruler, he would make only those people fall in love who could, either at once or after a proper amount of suffering, have their love returned; since he does not do this, it would seem proper to refuse to enter into his service. It does not seem as though you ought to love the company of a man who would lead you forth to battle and then when the fighting begins go over to the enemy and help him to defend himself against you. Therefore it is not advisable, my respected friend, for you to waste your days on love which for all the reasons already given we agree ought to be condemned. For if it deprives you of the grace of the Heavenly King, and costs you every real friend, and takes away all the honors of this world as well as every breath of praiseworthy reputation, and greedily swallows up all your wealth, and is followed by every sort of evil, as has already been said, why should you like a fool, seek for love, or what good can you get from it that will repay you for all these disadvantages? That which above all you seek in love—the joy of having your love returned—you can never obtain as we have already shown, no matter how hard you try, because no woman ever returns a man's love. Therefore, if you will examine carefully all the things that go to make up love, you will see clearly that there are conclusive reasons why a man is bound to avoid it with all his might and to trample under foot all its rules.

Now this doctrine of ours, which we have put into this little book for you will, if carefully and faithfully examined, seem to present two different points of view. In the first part we tried to assent to your simple and youthful request and did not wish, on this subject, to give in to our indolence; so we set down completely, one point after another, the art of love as you so eagerly asked us to do, and now that it is all arranged in the proper order, we hand it over to you. If you wish to practice the system, you will obtain, as a careful reading of this little book will show you, all the delights of the flesh in fullest measure; but the grace of God, the companionship of the good, and the friendship of praiseworthy men you will with good reason be deprived of, and you will do great harm to your good name, and it will be difficult for you to obtain the honors of this world.

In the latter part of the book we were more concerned with what might be useful to you, and of our own accord we added something about the rejection of love, although you had no reason to ask for it, and we treated the matter fully; perhaps we can do you good against your will. If you will study carefully this little treatise of ours and understand it completely and practice what it teaches, you will see clearly that no man ought to mis-spend his days in the pleasure of love. If you abstain from it, the Heavenly King will be more favorably disposed toward you in every respect, and you will be worthy to have all prosperous success in this world and to fulfill all praiseworthy deeds and the honorable desires of your heart, and in the world to come to have glory and life everlasting.

Therefore, Walter, accept this health-giving teaching we offer you and pass by all the vanities of the world, so that when the Bridegroom cometh to celebrate the greater nuptials, and the cry ariseth in the night you may be prepared to go forth to meet Him with your lamps filled and to go in with Him to the divine marriage, and you will have no need to seek out in haste what you need for your lamps, and find it too late, and come to the home of the Bridegroom after the door is shut, and hear His venerable voice.

Be mindful, therefore, Walter, to have your lamps always supplied, that is, have the supplies of charity and good works. Be mindful ever to watch lest the unexpected coming of the Bridegroom find you asleep in sins. Avoid then, Walter, practicing the mandates of love, and labor in constant watchfulness so that when the Bridegroom cometh He may find you wakeful; do not let worldly delight make you lie down in your sins, trusting to the youth of your body and confident that the Bridegroom will be late, since as He tells us Himself, we know neither the day nor the hour.